CW01500734

INTRODUCTION

This book is not about how to hit the tennis ball. It's about where to hit the ball, when, and why. It lays out the quickest and best way to raise your game to the next level. For recreational players—those between 3.0 and 4.0 in the National Tennis Rating Program (NTRP)—the single, most transformative step you can take is to develop a strategic approach to the game.

In this book, you will learn how to take advantage of the strengths in your game, how to minimize your weaknesses, and how to attack your opponent's game.

Most tennis players start by focusing on the mechanics of their strokes. That makes sense. If you can't hit the ball over the net and inside the lines, the rest doesn't really matter.

Later, when you're hitting the ball well, it's fun to keep working on your shots. All tennis players love to hit the ball.

Unfortunately, stroke improvement has a diminishing return. Early on you improve rapidly, but then the pace levels off. It can be frustrating to work, week after week, month after month, and not see any progress.

Developing your strategic understanding of the game completely changes that dynamic. It's difficult to exaggerate how much focusing on strategy can improve every aspect of your game.

At first glance, tennis is a marvelously simple game. All you have to do is hit the ball over the net and inside the lines one time more than your opponent does and you win the point. Do that often enough and you win the match.

In truth, however, tennis is endlessly complex. That's why it becomes a lifetime passion for so many of us. It's a demanding amalgamation of muscle memory, hand-eye coordination, geometric understanding, stamina, and split-second decision making.

Adding another layer of complexity, most of us model our games on professional tennis players. We see them win points by smacking the felt off the ball, going for the lines, serving aces, and hitting topspin lobs from outside the doubles alley. We want to play like that. The catch is we don't have unbelievable hand-eye coordination and don't practice eight hours a day.

Is it any wonder, then, that about 80 percent of points in a recreational match end with an unforced error?

That's right.

Eight out of 10 points—and often more—end because you or your opponent hits the ball into the net or out. When we come out of top in a match, we like to think that we won. It's probably more accurate to say that we didn't lose.

Winning Singles Strategy for Recreational Tennis Players

140 Tips and Tactics for Transforming Your Game

GERRY DONOHUE

If you want to come out on the winning side more often—and enjoy the game more—one strategy stands above all others for recreational tennis players: Reduce your unforced errors. Cutting your unforced errors by just a few per set can lead to an exponential leap in matches won.

When you play strategically, you recognize that every shot has a purpose. Shots are links in a chain. To reach the end, you can't have any breaks.

The following chapters are filled with strategies and tactics that you can adopt and adapt to improve your game. You don't need to apply all of them; use only the concepts that work for you. If altering the strategies better suits your game, go for it.

Playing strategically will make your game more consistent. You'll become a better competition and you'll have more fun.

BASIC STRATEGIC SKILLS

Players at every skill level benefit from approaching the game strategically. It forces you to think about how you play—about what you can and cannot do.

Strategy focuses your efforts and helps you make the most of your ability.

Still, to benefit from many of the concepts in this book, you need a base level of skills. As you incorporate strategic thinking into your game, these skills will rapidly improve.

(If you are NTRP 3.0 and above, you can skip this section.)

Keep the ball in play. The foundation of any successful tennis strategy is being able to hit the ball over the net and inside the lines one time more than your opponent does.

Consistency, however, is relative. At the beginner level, it can be enough to keep the ball in play for two shots; at higher levels, keeping the ball in play for 25 shots may be necessary to win the point.

You can never be too consistent. If you can keep hitting the ball back into the court, you will always be in the point.

Control the ball's direction and depth. You need to be able to steer the ball. That doesn't mean dropping it on a dime or even in a hula hoop, but being able to direct it into the deuce or ad court.

Controlling depth is more difficult than direction. Concentrate merely on hitting your shots beyond the service line.

Play with spin. Spin opens up a wide range of strategic possibilities. Topspin is the foundation of an effective baseline game. Your ball clears the net by several feet and still comes down inside the lines.

For a lot of players, underspin, or slice, is the natural stroke on the backhand. It can be a good strategic response to hard hitters and serve-and-volleyers, and it's the best stroke for approaching the net.

Hit with—some—power . Of all these skills, power is the least important. If you improve your consistency, control and spin, you will naturally develop the ability and confidence to hit the ball harder.

CUT DOWN YOUR UNFORCED ERRORS

If reducing unforced errors is such an effective strategy, why doesn't everybody do it? Here are three primary reasons.

Unaware of the importance. Most players have no idea of the huge impact of unforced errors on the game. If you were to ask the average recreational player how many of his points ended with a mistake, he'd probably guess fewer than half. In reality, it's 80 percent or more.

Stroke approach. We try to improve our consistency by improving our strokes. Few of us, though, have the proper technique or sufficient practice time to make our strokes bulletproof. All of us know tennis fanatics who've been playing all their lives and still can't hold their own in a rally of more than a few strokes.

Powerful role models. We see all the winners that the pros hit and want to do that, ignoring the fact that these are superb athletes whose sole focus in life is hitting a tennis ball. And here's a sobering fact: Despite their skill and talent, often more than half of the points in a pro match end in an unforced error.

You can't eliminate unforced errors, but you can reduce them. Cutting out just a few in each set can be the difference between winning and losing.

The key to reducing your unforced errors is to make it your strategic priority. Too often, in the heat of the match, we go for the big winner—and we miss. With one swing, we gift the point to our opponent. If, however, we don't give in to temptation and put the ball back in the court, we put the pressure back on our opponent.

A word of caution: It's not enough just to bunt the ball over the net. Your shots will land soft and short, a dangerous combination at any level of the game. Instead, concentrate on landing every shot past the service line and well away from the sidelines and the baseline.

KEEP IT DEEP

Billie Jean King reportedly once said that if she could hit every ball within a foot of the baseline, she would never lose. She was such a great player that it was a reasonable goal. For us, it's enough to settle for consistently landing the ball past the service line.

Although hitting balls past the service line may not appear to be particularly aggressive, in most cases it's enough to pin your opponent to the baseline.

Hitting the ball deep takes the initiative away from your opponent. If she's hitting every shot at or behind the baseline, she can't go for winners, attack your shots, or take control of the point. You, on the other hand, can take advantage of your consistency to lure her into an unforced error or a short ball.

As you become more consistent, aim deeper, but don't push it. For most of us, the deepest that you want to target is about six feet in front of the baseline. That gives you enough margin of error so your long balls will stay in and your short shots will still have some depth.

Hitting deep consistently requires topspin. Flat shots bring the net into play and to hit them with depth requires a risky amount of pace.

With topspin, you take the net out of the equation. And because topspin brings the ball back down into the court, you increase your control. Topspin also produces a high-bouncing ball, which can push your opponent behind the baseline and limit her ability to put pressure on you.

HIT CROSS-COURT

Hit at least 80 percent of your shots cross-court. You will reduce your unforced errors and increase the pressure on your opponent to try to win the point.

Court geometry rewards the cross-court shot. The net is 5 1/2 inches lower at the middle than at the lines. On the diagonal, the court is 4 1/2 feet longer. These differences may sound small but they have a huge impact because unforced errors decide so many points. By taking advantage of those increased margins for error, you dramatically improve your odds of winning the point.

"Hit cross-court" is also a simple strategy. You don't need to think about it. The game is much easier when you know what you're going to do.

Cross-court doesn't mean corner-to-corner, because you don't want to bring the baseline and the sideline come into play. Concentrate on hitting deuce-court-to-deuce-court and ad-court-to-ad-court.

As the cross-court rally plays out, you or your opponent will get antsy and try to end the point by hitting down the line. Don't let it be you. It's almost always a bad strategic decision. Not only is the geometry of the court against you, but changing the direction of the ball dramatically increases the chances of making an unforced error. And even if your down-the-line shot somehow finds the corner, you've opened up yourself for the cross-court reply.

POUND YOUR OPPONENT'S WEAKNESS

If you don't have a game that you can impose on your opponent, your best strategy is to expose the weaknesses in his game.

Start searching for his weaknesses in the warm-up. Does he avoid a stroke or run around it? Which way does he go when you hit the ball right at him? Does he hit a certain shot awkwardly? How does he move side to side? Does he move forward well? How does he hit high balls or low balls? Keep probing until you've located his weakness, and then target that weakness throughout the match.

Most recreational players have a weaker backhand, so we'll use it as an example of how to exploit a weakness.

Be unrelenting. Hit every shot that you can to his backhand. Do it until it feels unsportsmanlike, and then do it some more. Aim at least 80 percent of your first serves and all of your second serves at your opponent's backhand. During rallies, move the ball with the intention of getting to his backhand. Approaches go to the backhand. So do volleys.

Don't force it. Although you want to pound the weaker stroke, don't do it at your own expense. Stay within your game. Play consistently and strategically. If your opponent keeps running around his backhand to hit forehands, adapt your strategy and hit wide to his forehand. If he returns the ball, hit your next shot to his backhand.

Vary your spins. Hit low, biting slices and high, looping topspins. Many players have problems with high, soft balls to their backhand.

Keep the ball deep. A short ball can be a "get out of jail" card for your opponent, because he can follow it into the net. Land your shots beyond the service line.

Magnify your strength. Look for balls that you can run around and hit with your forehand. Points in which you're hitting your forehand to your opponent's backhand will end well for you.

Be predictable. Don't worry that he'll figure out that you're preying on his backhand. He probably encounters the same strategy in every match.

Pound away throughout the match. You may have heard that you shouldn't hit every ball to a weakness because you'll make it stronger; you should only prey on the weakness in key points. I disagree. The pressure of playing a match doesn't lend itself to improving a stroke. If your opponent has a bad backhand when the match starts, he's still going to have it when you finish. It's up to you to determine how much it hurts him in between.

HIT WITH PURPOSE

Hit every shot with a purpose. Every time you strike the ball, try to improve your position—either by gaining a better court position or forcing your opponent into a worse one.

One of the best ways to improve your position is to move forward after your shot, even if only a half a step. Not only do you increase the angles for your next shot, forcing your opponent to cover more court, you also return her ball back sooner, robbing her of time.

When rallying, strive to pit your strengths against your opponent's weaknesses. The most common example is maneuvering your opponent into a cross-court rally and hitting forehands to her backhand. There are numerous other tactics. Against a power baseliner, low, sliced backhands can induce a spate of unforced errors. Approaching on short balls can disrupt many players' games.

Even if you're a defensive baseline player, without an attacking edge, you can keep the pressure on your opponent by varying your shots and moving her along the baseline. If she's stooping and reaching for balls and running side-to-side, she won't be able to generate the power to take control of the point.

If you force your opponent to keep hitting good shots to beat you, she probably won't.

PROTECT YOUR BACKHAND

As much as you want to impose your strengths on a match, you also need to minimize your weaknesses. For most of us, that means protecting our backhand. A smart opponent will direct his serves, groundstrokes, and volleys at your backhand until you prove that it's a losing strategy.

Your first imperative on your backhand is to keep the ball in play. Don't give away points through unforced errors. Make your opponent hit another shot and another shot. Make him win the point.

Hit every backhand cross-court. This is your safest shot, and with most opponents you'll be hitting to their backhand.

When our backhand is under assault, many of us try to end the point quickly. Resist the urge. Going for a backhand winner often surrenders the point because it's a high-risk shot. Instead, play conservatively. Keep the ball in and make your opponent hit for the lines.

Focus on depth rather than power. If you can keep your opponent at or behind the baseline, he'll be hard-pressed to put pressure on your backhand.

In baseline rallies, shade toward the backhand side of the court to narrow your opponent's target area. Wait for a shot that lands short or near the center line, then run around and hit your forehand.

If your backhand is truly weak, nullify its impact by getting to the net. Serve and volley in your service games and chip and charge in your opponent's. Don't give him the opportunity to expose your backhand.

When you're on the defensive on your backhand, throw up a lob to relieve the pressure and give yourself time to regroup.

KEEP IT SIMPLE

Strategy for recreational players is not Xs and Os on a whiteboard court delineating the exact spot where you want to hit your shot to force a specific reply that allows you to hit a follow-up shot that swings the point in your favor. We're just not that good.

Recreational tennis strategy is amorphous; it's more mashed potatoes than French fries. While we can't put the ball on a dime or flawlessly change the direction of our shots, we can target sides of the court and get the ball beyond the service line with relative consistency.

Given these limitations, how should we approach strategic play?

Look upon strategy as more of a direction more than a directive. It's a way of playing, of adding a new dimension to your game. When you walk on the court, you have an idea of what you want to do. You have a catalog of key items to check off before the ball goes in play.

On service returns, for example, your catalog may consist of the following:

- Hit the ball cross-court.

- If the ball is on your forehand, return it with enough topspin to clear the net and get some measure of depth.

- If the ball is on your backhand, slice it back.

The list is simple, but powerful. Each of those items is within your skill set and gives you a more defined purpose beyond "get the ball back." At the same time, you aren't trying to do too much. You're not expanding your options based on the spin of the ball or the server's position on the court.

The same holds true during the run of play. If you have a short list of things you want to accomplish on each type of ball, you give yourself an immediate advantage.

Let's take a simple one: Hit every ball beyond the service line. That's straightforward and each of us should be doing it on every shot, but if you don't concentrate on this strategy, a lot of your shots will land short. Focusing on hitting balls beyond the service line gives you a goal, and often that's enough to achieve it.

ELIMINATING UNFORCED TACTICAL ERRORS

The unforced error that loses the point may not be the one you think it is.

On many points, our mistake is obvious. We hit our groundstroke long or into the net, we double-fault, or we spray the volley beyond the sideline. Other times, though, that final mistake was due to an earlier error.

Consider this point. Your opponent serves to your forehand in the deuce court. You return the ball up the line. She moves across the baseline, hits a cross-court backhand and follows it in. You scurry over, reaching the ball close to the sideline. Harried by her presence at the net, you go for a winner down the line—and miss.

At first glance, your error was going for the winner. You tell yourself that the next time she has you scrambling on your backhand, you will lob the ball deep or hit it cross-court. In reality, though, your error was returning her serve down the line. You immediately put yourself at a disadvantage and ceded control of the point to your opponent. The rest of the shots followed from that mistake.

By far, the most common unforced tactical error is hitting the ball short. When your groundstrokes land inside the service box, you gift too many advantages to your opponent. She can move in, hit an approach shot, and take the net. Or she can exploit her wider angle of reply to get you running side to side. Or she can move into the court to drive a groundstroke hard and deep, putting you in a tough defensive position. In each instance, you'll be hard pressed to avoid being forced into an "unforced" error.

Other common unforced tactical errors are missing too many first serves, failing to move to the center of your opponent's angle of reply, and not hitting volleys that put pressure on your opponent. In each case, you may hit one or two subsequent shots, but that early mistake will likely lead to your losing the point.

CONTROL FIRST, THEN POWER

When Andre Agassi burst onto the scene, there were lots of stories about how his father first taught him to hit the ball as hard as he could and only later focused on control. For a player as freakishly talented as Agassi, that sequence works; for the rest of us, it's backwards. You're much better off concentrating on your control and placement first. The power will come.

In recreational tennis (as I've mentioned before), most points are lost to unforced errors. Players go for too much. They try to hit a winner but more often find the net or hit the ball outside the lines. Killing the tennis ball can be a lot of fun, but not if it kills the point.

Focusing on control and placement not only improves your chances of winning the point today, it also gives you the tools to add power to your game tomorrow. Gaining control over your strokes reduces your unforced errors, allowing you to hit more balls in match conditions. You will become increasingly confident in your ability to strike the ball. And as you become more confident, you will find yourself naturally hitting the ball with more pace.

As an added benefit, hitting for placement engages you in the strategy of the game. Rather than simply trying to out-hit your opponent, you're looking to out-think him.

You learn how to move your opponent around the court, maneuver him to impose your strengths on his weaknesses, or take advantage of short balls to take control of the point.

COURT ZONES

Where you are on the court is more important in your shot selection than where your opponent is.

Most unforced errors occur because we try the wrong shot from the wrong spot on the court. We go for a winner when we're 10 feet outside the sideline. We attempt a drop shot from the baseline. Or we hit a running backhand down the line. Far more often than not, we're going to miss these shots. We're just giving away the point.

Basing your shot on your court position dramatically reduces your unforced errors and improves your winning percentage. You know when to play defensively, when to be more aggressive, and when to keep it in neutral.

Strategically, the tennis court can be divided into four zones: defensive, rally, offensive, and volley.

The defensive zone extends from about five feet behind the baseline to the back fence and stretches well outside doubles alleys.

You're at a positional disadvantage in this zone. You're so far behind the baseline or off the court that you can't generate the angles or power to put any pressure on your opponent. Still, so many of us go for a winner because we fear that any other shot will give our opponent an easy put-away.

When you're on the defensive, your best reply is to hit a high, deep shot and get back into a good court position. If you've been pushed back to fence, put up a deep lob to the backhand side. When you've been run outside the sidelines, hit a cross-court looper. Make your opponent try to put the ball away.

The rally zone is that narrow band along the baseline where you're confident that you can hold your own.

Here you can use your consistency to exert control over the points. Look to exploit your opponent's weaker strokes or to take advantage of her mistakes to improve your court position.

Maneuver the point so you're rallying from your stronger side and/or forcing your opponent to hit from her weaker side. When you get a short ball, go on the offense.

The offensive zone extends from the baseline to the service line. Here you're looking to put pressure on your opponent by moving in.

When you hit your approach shot, don't go for the outright winner. The offensive zone is actually a bad spot on the court to go for winners because you have less court to hit into and the net is more of a barrier. Instead, hit shots that force your opponent to play defense.

Hit the ball directly in front of you. You limit your opponent's angles and put yourself in a good position to volley.

The volley zone is the only area where you look to put the ball away, yet even here don't go for a winner on every shot.

You have the positional advantage in this zone, which extends from the service line to the net. The geometry of the court favors the player at the net. You have a wider angle of reply and you squeeze your opponent's response time.

If you can put the ball away, do. If you have a tough volley, though, be content to put the ball back in the court and make your opponent go for another shot.

GET YOUR FIRST SERVE IN

Getting your first serve in gives you a huge advantage because even if you never hit a flat, hard serve down the T, your opponent has to guard against it from the first game to your last.

Here are four keys to improve your first-serve percentage.

Hit your second serve first. Spin in your first serve. Serving with slice and/or topspin pulls the ball down into the box. In one fell swoop, you minimize double faults and keep your opponent from preying on your second serve.

Target the backhand. Hit 80 percent of your first serves at the backhand. Topspin serves to the backhand force your opponent to either hit the ball up around her shoulder, which is a difficult shot, or to step back, which robs her of any pace.

Put placement over power. Focus on hitting your locations, such as the corners of the service box or jamming the body.

Plan your second shot. You know where you're hitting your serve, so you have a fairly good idea of your opponent's return options. Plan your reply. For example, if you serve wide to the backhand, you can anticipate a cross-court return. As the match progresses, adapt both your service placement and movement to take advantage of your opponent's return patterns.

SMART RETURNS

The return of serve is an underappreciated shot, yet it's an important weapon in every player's arsenal. After all, the server has to hold her serve three times or more during each set; you only have to break her once.

The server has a lot of advantages. She gets to start the point when she's ready. She can decide where to direct her shot. And, if she misses the first one, she gets a second crack.

Here's how to neutralize those advantages and put pressure on the server.

Return every serve. Servers expect at least one free point every service game. Don't oblige. Make returning every serve into the court your primary focus. Force her to play out every point. Few things in tennis are more psychologically draining than having to fight for every one of your service games.

Go deep. Rather than going for a winner off the serve, return the ball deep. If you have the time, hit a deep topspin return. When you're facing a powerful serve, chip or bunt the ball back and let the server's power carry your shot beyond her service line.

Return cross-court. Cross-court returns limit your opponent's options. Her best shot is right back at you. Also returning cross-court removes any uncertainty from your strategy. You know where you're hitting on every return. Later in the match, if you're feeling comfortable and confident, vary your returns, but cross-court should remain your primary shot.

Recognize patterns. As the match progresses, you will pick up on your opponent's serving patterns, such as targeting your backhand on second serves or serving down the T at 30-love. Shade that way.

Adapt to difficult serves. If you're having trouble returning serve, vary your receiving position. On hard serves, take a couple steps back—the ball lose some pace and you'll have more time to prepare—or step in and block the ball back, using the server's power against her. Stepping in is also effective against slice or topspin serves, because you minimize the effect of the spin.

MIRROR YOUR OPPONENT

One of the best ways to build your shot consistency is to improve your court movement. If you are in the right place to hit the ball, you are going to hit it better.

Jimmy Connors was a prime example of the power of good movement. His groundstrokes were table-top flat and didn't leave a lot of room for error, but his movement was so good that he almost always had time to set up and hit the ball cleanly.

The key to getting in to the right position for the next shot is to start moving immediately after you hit the last one. Too often, we wait to see where our opponent hits the ball. Instead, play the percentages and move toward his most likely target on the court.

When you hit a cross-court groundstroke, for example, you don't want to slide all the way back to the center stripe, because your opponent's most likely reply is right back where you were.

On every shot, your best position is to bisect your opponent's angle of reply, which is the area of the court into which he can realistically hit the ball.

The easiest way to bisect the angle of reply is to mirror your opponent's position on the court. If he's standing halfway along the baseline in his deuce court, you want to be in the same spot in your deuce court.

Better players have wider angles of reply because they have more control over the ball and they can hit with more topspin.

You also want to position yourself to maximize your strengths and minimize your weaknesses. If you're strong at the net, step forward when you've hit a shot that will most likely draw a short or soft reply. If your backhand is a liability, shade toward that side to decrease your opponent's target area.

As the match progresses, you'll see patterns to exploit in your opponent's shot selection. Does he go down the line on his backhand? Are his service returns routinely cross-court? Does he always spin his second serves into your backhand?

Move to optimize your response to those tendencies. Leaning toward—or even just anticipating—the likely next shot can change the outcome of a half dozen or more points during a match.

Finally, as the match progresses, your opponent may realize how your movement is blunting his game and he'll adapt his game. Be ready to respond.

TAKING THE SHORT BALL

The only thing better than an unforced error by your opponent is a short ball. That's your invitation to move forward, hit an approach shot, and take the net. When you're at the net, even if you have only a serviceable volley, you are odds-on to win the point.

How short is short? On almost any ball that lands in your service box, move in. It's "almost any ball," because if your opponent hits a hard, flat ball that lands close to the service line, you may get stuck in no-man's land if you try to come in.

Anytime you force your opponent to turn her back to you, move forward.

Your approach shot is a means to the end of the point, not necessarily the end itself. Use it to set up your volley. Going for a winner on the approach is risky because you are moving as you hit the ball and the net is more of a barrier.

Your best backhand approach is a slice. The ball moves slower, giving you more time to get to the net, and it stays low, making it more difficult for your opponent to hit it cleanly.

On the forehand, most of us don't have a good slice, so your best option is hard topspin. The spin will lift the ball over the net and bring it back down in the court, and the power of the shot will put your opponent under pressure.

Approaching directly in front of you limits your opponent's response options. His best shot is to go back at you—or over your head.

Once you've gained the net, don't squander the opportunity by being impatient. If you get an easy ball, put it away. If your opponent hits a good shot, hit a reply that forces her to hit an even better one.

SMART VOLLEYS

You're at the net. Now what? Here are seven strategic volleying concepts.

Placement over pace. Pace is difficult to control. Taking pace off your volley will improve your consistency. Softer, well-placed volleys also force your opponent to move forward, lift the ball over the net, and generate her own pace—and to do all that with you waiting at the net.

Short-angled volleys. When you can put the ball away, hit a short, angled volley. It's a safe shot and difficult for your opponent to reach.

Volley straight ahead. When you can't put volley away, hitting directly in front of you puts you in the center of your opponent's angle of reply. Volleying cross-court opens up the court for your opponent.

Low down. The key on low volleys is to get lower than the ball. Hit the ball back deep and over the middle of the net.

High winner. When you get a high volley, put it away. It's as close to a gift that you will get on a tennis court.

Follow your ball. Move in the direction of the ball after you hit the volley. If you volley straight ahead, move forward. If you angle the ball to the right or left, slide in that direction. Always bisect your opponent's angle of reply.

Watch for the lob. When you're at the net, you want to lean forward to step into the shot and put the ball away. As a result, you're vulnerable to the lob. Study your opponent during the match to anticipate when she likes to lob.

WHAT'S YOUR SHOT TOLERANCE?

B uilding your shot tolerance is critical to developing your strategic tennis game.

Shot tolerance is the number of shots you can hit in a rally while remaining focused and comfortable. Most recreational players have a surprisingly low shot tolerance—as few as three or four strikes of the ball. After that, we become anxious about our ability to stay in the rally. Maintaining our concentration becomes difficult and we start looking for ways to end the point. Unfortunately, the most likely way we'll do that is by losing it.

Your opponent has a shot tolerance too, although she's probably unaware of the concept. You can use that to your advantage. If you build your shot tolerance above hers, she will be the one going for the ill-timed winners.

Shot tolerances pop up all the time when two players end up in a cross-court backhand rally. They're doing what they want to do— hitting to their opponent's weakness. Theoretically, each player should keep doing it, but one player is going to snap. They'll either change the ball's direction or amp up the power. Neither is a good idea.

Increasing your shot tolerance is simple. It's the same way we learn how to tolerate anything. Build it up. First, determine your current shot limit. At what number of shots do you start to feel anxious about the point? Then focus on extending that tolerance one shot at a time. Merely by being aware of it, you'll find that your shot tolerance climbs.

Your shot tolerance will eventually extend beyond the limits of almost all recreational points, giving you the security of knowing that you can keep hitting the ball back until your opponent reaches her limit.

THE TWO THINGS YOU CAN CONTROL
ON THE COURT

A fter countless hours of tennis lessons, assiduous reading of dozens of tennis books, and more than 20 years of Tennis magazine, the best piece of instruction that I've ever received wasn't even directed at me.

A friend and I were playing on public courts in Washington, D.C. On the adjacent court, a brother and sister were hitting the ball so beautifully that we spent minutes at a time just watching. We spoke with them afterwards. He'd been a professional tennis player, playing in some doubles tournaments on the ATP Tour, and she was a top-flight collegiate player.

After one particularly spirited rally in which they kept ramping up the power until she mishit a forehand, he called across the net to her, "The only things you can control are your contact point and follow-through."

I'm not going to claim that time stood still or that a beam of sunlight suddenly broke through the clouds, but that concept instantly resonated and has stuck with me ever since. It is my primary self-correction device when my game starts to go off the rails.

We think that we have a lot of control over our tennis game and the tennis court. We don't.

You don't control your opponent, and he accounts for half of everything that happens on the court. You can influence him through your shot selection and consistency—forcing him deep or getting him on the run—but you can't control what he does with the ball.

At the same time, you don't completely control over your own strokes. You don't always have the time to set up for each shot, measure your backswing, and hit a balanced stroke (that's called golf.) Depending on your opponent's shot, you may be hitting a groundstroke above your shoulders, chasing a shot outside the doubles alley, or scampering forward to pick up a drop shot. In each instance, you have to adapt your stroke to the realities of the ball.

Yet, as that former pro said, you can control your contact point and follow-through, and those are arguably the most important components of the stroke.

Regardless of how hard, soft, or angled your opponent's shot is, you almost always have the opportunity to hit it at your intended contact point. You may have to abbreviate or even eliminate your backswing, but you can still meet the ball where you want. It may not always be the same place or the ideal spot, but if it's the spot you intend, you'll be able to hit the ball cleanly.

Your follow-through is critical to imparting depth, spin, and height on the ball. Regardless of how hurried every other aspect of the stroke may be, you can almost always complete your follow-through, which allows you to reasonably return most shots.

PLAYING THE PERCENTAGES

Tennis is a game of risk and reward. To play well and win matches, you need to strike a balance.

Unforced errors are by far your biggest risk. In many games at this level, every point is decided by an unforced error. In entire sets, there may be less than a half dozen winners.

Conversely, it's also risky to be so focused on not making errors that you bunt back every ball. Although you're forcing your opponent to hit a lot of balls, if you continually hit short, soft shots, you will be on your back foot throughout the match and at the wrong end of the score at the end.

The key to limiting risks—and maximizing your reward—is to play the percentages. As professional gamblers know, the subtlest shift in the odds—even to just 51 to 49 percent—can be enough for you to come out on top.

Here are five steps to improving your odds of winning the match.

Hit the ball deep. When you keep your opponent at or behind the baseline, she can't put any consistent pressure on you. She can't hit winners or generate enough pace to attack you. If she starts to hit with more power, she'll increase her risks and her unforced errors will mount.

Keep your opponent moving. Most players don't hit the ball as well on the run. Making your opponent run—either along the baseline or up and back—tilts the percentages your way. You don't need to hit close to the lines. Just hit the ball with enough of an angle to force her to go get it.

Take the net. Even if you are not an adept volleyer, the odds are in your favor when you're at the net. Whenever you get a short ball, move forward and put pressure on your opponent.

Stop her from taking the net. Hitting the ball deep keeps your opponent from moving in. If she does come forward, a lob will force her back.

Have a plan. Taking the court with a game plan is your best percentage play. Knowing what you want to do—and what you want to stop your opponent from doing—gives you a decided edge from the first point until the last.

PLAYING STRENGTH TO WEAKNESS

Several years ago, Andy Roddick defeated Roger Federer in a three-set match at the Sony Ericsson Open. The match turned on the third game in the third set. Tied at 1-1, Roddick hit four searing forehand winners to break Federer's serve. He then served out to win the set and the match.

What was so striking in that pivotal game was that Federer continued to hit to Roddick's forehand despite the American's blasting one, two, three, and then four shots past him. He did that despite knowing that Roddick's forehand was by far his stronger stroke.

During the changeover after that game, one of the commentators said, "You always want to make your opponent beat you with his weakness, never his strength, even if you are Roger Federer."

Every player has weaknesses. In most cases, it's the backhand, especially the high backhand. For others it may be a balky overhead, a forehand that lands short, or limited court movement.

As you warm up and play the first few games, figure out your opponent's weaknesses and then spend the rest of the match forcing her to try to beat you with them.

THERE IS NO PLAN B

Always play your game. No matter how badly you're getting beaten, don't dump your strategy. It's your best hope for turning the match around.

You'll often hear TV commentators talk about switching to plan B. That doesn't make any sense. Your plan A maximizes your strengths. Whatever you do best, that should be what you bring to the court. Why, then, would you switch away from it? Why would you go to plan B? If you can't beat your opponent's plan A with your plan A, why would you be able to do it with your plan B?

That said, you're not on the court by yourself. You need to understand your opponent's strategy and respond to it. Your strategic decision making must be based on how you and your opponent are playing.

With each opponent, figure out which components of your strategy to emphasize and which ones to keep in your racquet bag. Adhere to your strategic fundamentals—reduce unforced errors, hit the ball deep, take the net, etc.—but be flexible around the edges. Maybe you need to hit the ball with more spin, approach the net on balls that land a little deeper in your court, or run around your backhand.

Adapt until you start to make too many errors. Don't damage your own game to hurt your opponent's.

If you push your game as far as you can and your opponent still has the upper hand, focus on his game and what you can do to disrupt it. If, for example, his big groundstrokes are blowing you off the court, hit some moonballs. Is his consistency from the baseline better than yours? Take the net. Keep experimenting—within your skill set—to force him to take more risks than he wants.

Adapt your game to the flow of match. On your serve, for example, your opponent will start to return better as he grooves to the speed and spin. When that happens, adjust your delivery. Hit with more spin or move around your locations.

In changeovers or between the sets, analyze the progress of the match. What are you doing that hurts your opponent? What is he doing that hurts you? What can you do about it? What is the match flow? Are you taking control or ceding it? What do you need to do to impose your game?

PATIENCE IS A VIRTUE

Tennis has evolved into a fast-paced power game. Recreational players, weaned on powerful racquets, hard courts, and the precision hitting of the pros, prefer the big serve and big groundstroke game. Most of us, however, don't have the skills for the big game. As a result, the patient hitter who consistently hits the ball deep into the court can flourish in the recreational game.

Patience is a potent weapon against every type of opponent.

Big hitters thrive by ratcheting up the power in a rally, hitting the ball harder with each shot. Typically, the points are over within three or four strokes, most often with someone's unforced error.

Rather than giving into their pressure, bleed it off. Focus on hitting deep. Slice the ball. Hit rolling topspin. Moonball or even lob. Big hitters don't like long rallies. With each additional stroke, their impatience and odds of missing increase exponentially.

Patience also works against serve-and-volley players. At our level, they tend to rely more on intimidation than a deft touch at the net. They win a lot of points without even hitting a volley because their flustered opponents immediately go for a risky passing shot.

Instead, stay calm. Don't try to pass right away. Make them win the point. Vary the spin and pace of your shots. Soft, underspin shots can wreak havoc for a fair-to-middling volleyer, especially if the ball dips below the level of the net. Conversely, a good lob can pull them away from the net, taking them out of their preferred game.

Even against the pusher, patience can be a powerful weapon. This may seem counter intuitive, because pushers appear to be the most patient players out there. In reality, they are more about mind games than endurance. Pushers want you to believe that they can hit back every shot in order to goad you into going for a winner.

Turn the tables on them. Playing a patient game guts their strategy. Hit deep topspin shots. Now, rather than counting on you to lose points, they have to win them, but their game isn't designed to do that.

IMPROVE YOUR COURT MOVEMENT

Most recreational tennis players have a wheelhouse. When the ball is in your wheelhouse, you can hit it cleanly and hard and with confidence. It's your rally stroke. The more shots you hit in your wheelhouse, the more points you'll win.

The rub, obviously, is that your opponent is unlikely to hit the ball where you want it. She's trying to keep her shots out of your wheelhouse.

So, if the ball won't come to your wheelhouse, you have to take your wheelhouse to the ball. Here are some tips to do that.

Commit Yourself. Get up on your toes as soon as she tosses the ball on her serve and stay there until the end of the point. This isn't a skill to develop; it's a commitment to make. Do it and you will immediately see huge returns in your court coverage and match results.

One of the best ways to get up on your toes is to split step just as your opponent starts her forward swing. Wherever you are on the court, even if you are out of position, split-stepping gives you the best chance to reach your opponent's shot.

Cover the options. After you hit your shot, move immediately to the middle of your opponent's angle of return. The easiest way to do that is to mirror her position on the court. If, for example, she is hitting from a couple feet inside the deuce court sideline, you want to stand a couple feet inside the sideline in your own deuce court.

Learn her tendencies. As you come to know your opponent's patterns, you can anticipate her shots and customize your court position. Does she target your backhand on the serve? Does she hit her backhands short? Is she slow coming in to the net? Use your analysis of her game to guide where you move. You'll be amazed at how quickly your anticipation will improve with a little practice.

Get in shape. To reach every ball from the first game to match point, you have to be fit. Again, this is a commitment, but it pays off. Nothing is more demoralizing for your opponent than your getting to every ball. Frustrated, she will often start to over-hit or go for too fine a shot, and she'll play her herself out of the match.

MOVE IN HALF A STEP AT A TIME

Next time you play, look down. Where you stand on the court when you hit your groundstrokes has a significant impact on your shots and your game.

Most recreational players set up three or four feet behind the baseline. We're comfortable there. We have more time to react to our opponent's shots. Not only does their ball have to travel farther, but it's moving slower when it reaches us.

The trade-off of playing that far back is we're hard pressed to put any pressure on our opponent. Not only do our shots lack pace, but our angle of reply is constrained. We pretty much have to hit into the middle third of the court.

To pressure your opponent, you have to get closer to the baseline.

During hitting sessions and in matches, commit to setting up nearer to the baseline. You don't need to emulate Andre Agassi and stand flush on the line, but see how close you can get and still maintain your comfort level and consistency.

Start with half a step. Hold that depth as you rally. Make a point of returning there if you're pushed back. At first it will be difficult to avoid retreating to your old position.

When you're closer to the baseline, your opponent's shots will arrive sooner and be moving faster, so you have to prepare early. Stay on your toes and anticipate where she'll hit the ball. Shorten your backswing if you have to. As you grow used to her pace, you'll be able to lengthen the backswing.

Focus on control rather than pace. You'll naturally hit the ball harder because you'll be using her pace against her. Concentrating on control will also allow you to probe your newly available angles on the court.

Once you're playing consistent tennis from this new spot, take another half step forward and acclimate yourself again. Keep moving forward until you just can't get comfortable. At that point, take a half step back.

THE BEST THING SINCE SLICED BREAD

When I first got into tennis, my favorite player was Mats Wilander. His game epitomized how I wanted to play--consistent, smart, dogged, and winning. The foundation of his game was topspin off both sides.

After several years on tour, though, he added a slice backhand to his arsenal. It seemed strange because he was so successful, but he recognized that he needed the flexibility that it brought to his game. A few years later, he reached #1.

Incorporating slice groundstrokes into your game, off both wings, can push your game to the next level. Slice is relatively safe to hit, can pose problems for the opposition, is a good defensive option when you've been pulled off the court, and offers a great change of pace.

Slice comes in several flavors.

Attacking slice. When you hit a sharp slice, the ball skids low off the court. Returning that ball can be difficult. Often, your opponent's reply will be short, giving you the opportunity to move forward and take the net.

The floater. When your opponent is dictating the pace with heavy shots, a high, floating slice can throw off his rhythm.

Recovery shot. When you're pulled outside the doubles alley, slice gives you a longer reach and the underspin carries the ball over the net. In addition, a sliced ball floats, giving you time to get back into position.

Passing shot. Most players drive their passing shots, but a slice is an effective option when your opponent takes the net. A low slice can elicit a netted volley because the underspin drives your opponent's reply downward. It's also a good change of pace.

Return of serve. When all you can do is get your racquet on a big serve, blocking the ball with underspin is usually enough to get the ball back and deep.

Sliced approach. On a short ball, your best shot is to slice your approach. The ball skips low off the court, forcing your opponent to hit up on the ball. Most of us are comfortable with slicing on the backhand, but it's also a good idea to develop your forehand slice. When two righties are playing, a forehand sliced approach targets your opponent's backhand.

WHEN YOU DON'T VOLLEY WELL

Fundamental to a successful singles strategy is moving forward on a short ball and taking control of the net. Given the geometry of the tennis court, you have the advantage when you're at the net. You put your opponent under pressure, give him less time to return the ball, and narrow his shot options.

What do you do, though, if your net game is truly bad? What if you don't like to come forward because you couldn't volley a beach ball into the ocean? Still come in.

Regardless of your volleying prowess, you're almost always better off taking the net. It often doesn't seem like that because we tend to magnify the points we lose at the net. At the end of the match we may feel that we lost most of the net points, but that's usually not the case.

The next time you play a match, track the number of times you come into the net and the number of points you win. Count your volley winners, points won on your approaches and your opponent's unforced errors, which will likely account for the lion's share of your points. You'll be surprised at how high your overall winning percentage is.

The best way to improve your net play is to improve your approach shot. A good approach puts you in position to hit an easy volley. Approach only on balls that land short enough for you to volley the next ball. Hit your approach directly in front of you. It's your easiest shot, and you force your opponent to create an angle to pass you.

When you're at the net, crowd it. You may feel vulnerable to the lob, but you improve your chances of keeping your volley in the court.

Don't try to do too much with your volleys. All you have to do is block the ball back. At best, you'll hit a winner. At worst, you'll force your opponent to hit another shot.

Finally, be real. If you keep coming in on short balls and your opponent keeps passing you like a BMW on the autobahn or you're repeatedly chunking your volleys into the net, stop coming in. Don't hold to a losing strategy solely because it should be a winning one.

Keep working on your volley, though, because it's a winning strategy.

NO SURPRISES

When was the last time your opponent caught you by surprise on the tennis court? When did she hit a shot that you never expected? When did she flummox you? It's probably been quite a while.

If you look over the history of your competitive tennis, you can probably count on one hand the number of times an opponent's shot successfully caught you off-guard.

Why, then, do we try to hit flummoxing shots? You know the ones: the inexplicable change of direction in the middle of a rally; the out-of-the-blue drop shot; or the backhand overhead down the line. The true surprise would be actually winning the point. Instead we end up gifting it to our opponent.

Tennis has a finite number of sound strategic responses determined by the ball's pace, spin, and depth and your court position.

A medium-paced ball bouncing flush on the service-line T gives you the widest possible range of responses, yet there's not much you can do to surprise your opponent. Your best shot is to hit the ball deep to your opponent's weaker wing and approach the net. It's simple yet effective.

At the opposite extreme is a shot that pins us deep in the corner. Our options are severely limited, yet we often try to whip a Nadal-like cross-court winner or—even better—to bend a shot around the post. Instead, put up a defensive lob and get back into position. It's simple yet effective.

WINNING THE KEY POINTS

Tennis matches are won and lost on a few key points. Play those points better than your opponent and your winning percentage will soar.

Tennis books (including this one) tell you to focus on every point regardless of the score. Although that's a worthwhile goal, it isn't going to happen. Your attention is going to wax and wane, and so is your opponent's. Accept that reality and concentrate on winning the points in the match that are truly decisive.

What are the key points? Obviously break points (regardless of whether you are serving or returning), game points, set points, and match points are decisive, but are there others?

In his book Winning Ugly, Brad Gilbert argues that several other points in a game are critical. He calls these the setup points, because they set up a game point. They are 30-15, 15-30, 30-love, love-30, 30-30, and deuce. He asserts that if you get more ad-point opportunities—or prevent your opponent from getting them—you will probably win the match.

Gilbert's insight can have a profound impact on your game. If you amp up your focus on the setup points, which your opponent probably considers run of the mill, you have a hidden advantage.

Plan prior to the match how you will play the decisive points. Determining your strategy up front increases your chances of winning these points because you'll know what you want to do.

Emphasize your strengths. If you're a consistent baseliner, stay back and rally. Don't serve and volley or go for backcourt winners. Don't lose these points; force your opponent to win them.

Stay in the moment. The points last only a few shots. You can focus your concentration for that long.

Be patient. Most recreational players try to end decisive points too quickly. They go for the big serve or the winner on the return. Instead, keep the ball in play and let your opponent surrender to the temptation.

FOUR SHOTS TO AVOID

Have you ever gone out to play a match after watching the pros on television? Were you inspired by their power and athleticism? Did you feel like you were ready to raise your game?

It's a common reaction to watching the pros, but it's also unrealistic. The pros play an entirely different game. Sure, the court is the identical size, the balls bounce just as high, and the rules are the same, but that's where any similarity ends.

The pros are freaks of nature. Through a combination of profound physical gifts and tens of thousands of hours of practice, they can do things with a tennis ball that the rest of us can't even comprehend. They are the computer and we are the abacus.

Many years ago, at the pro tournament in Washington, D.C., one "lucky" fan got to play a game against a pro. The fan was given a love-40 lead on the pro's serve. The pro proceeded to hit five straight aces. The fan never even got close to the ball. While this may say a lot about that pro's sense of fun, it also speaks to how good these guys are.

So, while you may feel inspired when you head out onto the court after watching the pros play, don't get carried away. Many of the shots they hit should not be part of your arsenal.

Here are the four shots to avoid.

Drop shot from the baseline. For players like Djokovic and Federer, this has become a go-to shot; for the rest of us, it should be a stay-away shot. The drop shot is difficult enough to hit when we're at the net. As we move back, the difficulty increases exponentially

Backhand smash put-away. If you come into the net, you're going to get lobbed to your backhand side. The urge is to try to put away that ball with a hard smash. Fight the urge. The backhand smash is the hardest shot in tennis. Unless you practice it regularly, you'll miss. Instead, let the ball drop a little and hit it like a high volley, going for angle or depth, and set up for the next shot.

Running topspin lob. This is one of the prettiest shot in tennis and is so much fun to hit. Watching the ball whip over your opponent's head and drop inside the baseline is almost a religious experience. Unfortunately, it is also often a miracle. Most of us don't recognize how often we miss this shot. If you were to chart your running topspin lobs, you would find a large number landed short, giving your opponent an easy put-away; another bunch went long; and you shanked many of the rest. You're better off putting up a defensive lob and getting back into position.

Tweenie. Enough said.

WORK YOUR WAY INTO THE MATCH

In the warm-up before playing a match, most of us hit some groundstrokes for a couple of minutes, come to the net for a few volleys, try a few overheads and lobs, hit a dozen or so serves, and then spin the racquet. That's hardly sufficient to get your engine revving and your mind into the match.

Here's how to use the warm-up to give yourself an early leg-up.

Tune your spins. When you hit your groundstrokes in the warm-up, exaggerate your topspin and your slice. Get a feel for your spins early. Most players spend the first few games dialing in their shot velocity. Spinning from the start gives you a decided advantage.

Find your depth. Focus on the depth of your shots in the warm-up and early in the match. Commit to hitting every ball beyond the service line.

Focus on your second serve. As with the groundstrokes, use your practice serves to find your spins and your placements. Hit a couple of hard serves, but get the feel for your second serve. Early in the match, hit only second serves.

Watch your opponent's strokes. What is his weakest stroke? Players tend to be tentative with their problem stroke early on. Pick on it from the start and you may prevent him from gaining confidence in the stroke for the entire match.

Avoid unforced errors. Consistency takes on even more importance during the first few games when both of you are feeling your way into the match. Keep the ball high over the net and away from the sidelines.

Go for the first break. Your opponent's first service game is often your best opportunity for a break. Don't give him any free points. Put every return in play. Force him to win every point.

FIXING A LOSING GAME

When you are on the wrong end of the score, your first priority is to determine why. Are you playing poorly, making unforced errors, hitting the ball short, or just not playing smart? Or is your opponent on her game, taking control of the points and the match? In the first instance, you need to look to your game; in the second, you need to focus on hers.

Some days your game is off. You hit your groundstrokes too long or too short, the sidelines seem to encroach into the court, and your strategic thinking is fuzzy. To get back into the match, you need to take control of your game.

Play more conservatively. Hit your groundstrokes cross-court, accentuating topspin to clear the net and to bring the ball back into the court. Don't flirt with either the sidelines or the baseline; instead, focus solely on getting the ball beyond the service line.

Come into the net on short balls. Approach on every short ball. You shift the odds in your favor when you're at the net.

Put in every first serve. Reduce the velocity of your serve and increase the spin. Even though you're playing it safe, most opponents will continue to respect your first serve and stay back.

Block your service returns. Hit them cross-court and deep. Use slice. Focus more on getting the ball back than being aggressive.

Now, what should you do if you're playing well but still losing?

Add more height and depth to your groundstrokes. Pushing your opponent back can disrupt her game. She can no longer hit pressing shots.

Attack her weaker wing. All you need is a little breathing space. Directing all of your shots—within reason—to her weaker side can bleed off some pressure.

Vary spin and pace. Upset your opponent's rhythm by giving her different types of balls. Many players have problems with looping shots or moonballs, not knowing whether to attack or backtrack.

Move her around. Another way to upset an opponent's rhythm is to get her running. If she is moving back and forth or up and back, she'll have problems hitting clean, forcing shots.

Lengthen the points. At the recreational level, players can't stay at a high level of play for long periods of time. By extending the points and the games, you give your opponent the opportunity to tumble off her plateau and return to the level where you can impose your game.

ANTICIPATION

A nticipation isn't an innate trait. It's a learned skill that you can develop to give yourself a significant advantage on the court.

All of us have some level of anticipation. After playing tennis for only a short time, you can tell where your opponent is hitting the ball, how hard she hit it, and what kind of spin she put on it.

Your advantage multiplies, though, when you can anticipate your opponent's shots before she hits them.

In every match, study your opponent's shot patterns. Every player has patterns. (The premise of this book is for you to develop the most effective patterns for your skills.)

During the first few games of the first set, pay attention to what your opponent does in specific situations. When does she hit a cross-court forehand? Cross-court backhand? A shot down the line? Where does she aim her first serve? Second serve? Return? Does she come in on a short ball or does she retreat to the baseline?

Merely by paying attention, you can quickly get a sense of her patterns. When pressed on her backhand, for example, she lobs, but on her forehand , she goes down the line on her forehand. Keeping track of her tendencies will give you a strategic edge.

MIX UP THE PACE

Mixing up the pace and spin of your shots is a great way to throw off your opponent's game. For most of us the goal of "never letting your opponent see the same ball twice" is unrealistic, but we can vary our shots without undermining our consistency.

Most recreational players play best when fed a steady diet of similar shots—either in terms of pace or spin. Steady power is especially appealing, because a lot of players have trouble generating their own.

While it can be fun to engage in a long cross-court rally, smacking one ball after another, take your foot off the accelerator every so often. Keep hitting cross-court, but float a ball deep, then maybe flatten out the next one.

If your opponent doesn't know what's coming, she can't get comfortable. If you can get her to focus on what you might do, she won't be able to concentrate on what she should do.

The cornerstone of this strategy is to not hit dramatically different shots. You don't upset your own game in an effort to upend hers. Only vary your shots when you have the opportunity.

Here are some simple guidelines:

- If the ball is high to your backhand, hit a slice.
- If it's chest high to your forehand, roll a high topspin shot.
- If it's low and hard, just get it back.
- Hit the occasional moonball or even put up a lob.
- On your serve, vary your pace and spin to prevent your opponent from grooving her returns.

LOVE THE LOB

The lob may be the most underutilized shot in the recreational game, but it's an integral weapon in the strategic player's arsenal. A well-placed and well-timed lob can negate an opponent's positional advantage and reverse the momentum in the point.

When you are at a disadvantage on the court, a deep lob can quickly change the dynamic. You have the chance to get back into position and restart the point.

Anytime you are pulled off the court, a lob should be your first option. Your chances of driving a forcing shot from outside the court are low, while the risk of making an unforced error is high.

The key to a successful lob is depth. You want to land the ball beyond the service line. Even if your opponent gets under it, hitting an overhead that far from the net isn't easy.

Lob to your opponent's backhand. The backhand overhead is one of the most difficult in the game and even one that's hit well is difficult to put away. Many players hit their backhand overheads cross-court, because there's more court to hit into, so shade that way.

If your lob gets beyond your opponent and she turns to chase it down, move forward. The advantage is now yours.

If you get lobbed and you can't reach it for an overhead, get behind the ball and lob or hit a looping forehand. Get the point back on an even keel.

IF YOU MASTER ONE SHOT

Develop your backhand. It's the single most important stroke in your game because it's the one your opponents will target. You don't need to hit winners off your backhand, but you need to be able to hold your own.

Your backhand can—and probably will—be your weaker shot, but it can't be a weak shot. You have to be able to hit it back in the court consistently.

You don't need power as much as you need depth. You probably won't hit a lot of winners by hitting your backhands deep, but you'll win a lot of points.

Work on your backhand until you can camp out in the ad court (if you're right handed) and hit cross-court shots all day long. Focus on hitting with topspin. It provides the greatest margin for error and gives your ball a little kick off the bounce. Additionally topspin gives you some variety; you can flatten it out to add some pace or put a lot of air under the ball to slow down the point.

Slice is another great option on the backhand. Not only is it the natural swing path for a lot of players, it's a safe shot that will keep you in the point.

The key with the backhand is not to try to do too much. Stay patient. Focus on keeping the ball in and keeping it deep. Let your opponent be the aggressor, because that often leads to unforced errors.

REMEMBER HOW THEY USED TO HIT TOPSPIN

When you picture your topspin groundstroke, don't channel Rafael Nadal. He punishes the ball, hitting with such power and spin that from a dozen feet behind the baseline he can slug it past the best players in the world.

Instead, think back to the topspin hitters of a decade or two ago, such as Mats Wilander or Arantxa Sanchez Vicario. These players hit their topspin groundstrokes with little intention of winning the point outright. They used their groundstrokes to probe for weaknesses, maneuver their opponent around, look for an opening, gain control of the point, or—best of all—elicit an unforced error.

They are good role models. Their shots cleared the net by a wide margin and landed deep. Although they moved the ball from side to side more than most of us probably should, they didn't flirt with the lines. They won with consistency and depth.

Forget about whipping the ball past your opponent from the baseline or hitting it at such an acute angle that he can't reach it without trespassing on the adjacent court. Instead, hit topspin that clears the net by several feet, lands beyond the service line, and stays away from the lines. Concentrate on safety and depth rather than power.

Hitting topspin builds your confidence, and having confidence in a shot makes a huge difference. You will become much steadier player, able to hit your shots regardless of the match situation.

THE BEST PRACTICE FOR VOLLEYING

Recreational players tend to avoid the net because the volley is often a weak link in our game. A big reason for that is we don't work to improve them. We limit our volleying practice to the few balls we hit during the pre-match warm-up or occasional forays forward during hitting sessions.

The irony is the volley is actually one of the easiest shots in the game. It's much less complicated than hitting from the baseline or serving. You need to do little more than block the ball back.

I recently came across a simple practice that will drastically improve anyone's volleying. Rather than focusing on the step-by-step mechanics of the shot or the positioning of the feet, this practice focuses on hitting the ball—over and over and over again.

Here's how to do it: Stand three or four feet from a wall and hit volleys. That's it. Volley until you miss; then pick up the ball and volley some more. You can focus on forehand volleys, backhand volleys, or both. Volley for as long as you want to or as long as you can. You'll be amazed at how quickly you improve.

This practice works because it trains you to watch the ball all the way to your racquet. If you don't, you will miss-hit the volley and have to start again. This heightened hand-eye coordination transfers onto the court. When you're in a match and at the net, you'll be amazed at how well you volley.

DON'T WATCH YOUR OPPONENT

You've probably heard that you should watch our opponent to get a jump on where she's going to hit the ball. Although that strategy works for the pros, it doesn't play well at the recreational level.

The primary reason to not watch your opponent is that you need to focus all of your attention on the ball. Most of us have enough trouble with that simple task. Complicating it with another one is counterproductive.

Second, when you're playing strategically, you have more than enough information to anticipate your opponent's shot selection. From the start, you'll know where she should hit the ball. As the match progresses, you'll figure out where she will hit the ball.

You want to cover her most threatening option. If, for example, she has a chance to put the ball wide to your backhand, lean in that direction. If she's hitting an approach, figure that she will hit it directly in front of her. She may not hit the "correct" shot, but you want to make sure you're ready for it. Any other shot won't be quite as dangerous.

THE SOFT VOLLEY HAS FINALLY ARRIVED

For most of the history of the game, hitting the volley hard and deep was your best choice. The small, heavy wooden racquets made passing shots more difficult, so if you put your volley deep into your opponent's court, you were odds-on to win the point.

Today's bigger, more powerful racquets and sticky strings have closed those odds. You still have the advantage when you're at the net, but it's nowhere near what it once was.

Enter the soft volley. It's not a drop volley, which is a difficult shot to hit. With the soft volley, you block the ball into your opponent's court. It lands without much pace or depth.

For a number of reasons, the soft volley is a good alternative for recreational players.

It's easier to hit. You only need to put your strings on the ball.

It's safer. How many times have you hit a deep volley long or put an angled volley wide? You had the advantage and then you gave it away. With the soft volley, you aren't playing near the lines. The ball lands in the middle of the court.

It's tougher to return. The soft bounce keeps the ball low—forcing your opponent to hit up. There's nothing on the ball—making him generate the power. And he's moving as he hits—increasing his degree of difficulty.

It limits his options. As the distance between you and your opponent shrinks, his options decrease. Angles tighten and pace becomes problematic. His best shots are to hit right at your body or to lob, so be prepared for either. Against almost any other shot, you are well positioned to angle away a volley.

LET YOUR OPPONENT SERVE FIRST

If you win the spin of the racquet at the beginning of the match, let your opponent serve first.

This choice has no downside.

What is her best outcome if she serves first? She wins her serve, which she's supposed to do, so her best outcome is breaking even.

What do you gain by letting her serve first?

Her first service game is your best opportunity to break her. She won't be fully warmed up and into the match. Breaking her early will give you an advantage that can set the tone for the rest of the match.

That means, of course, that you need to be laser-focused with the first point. Commit to getting every return back in the court—and deep. Keep as much pressure on your opponent as you can. Don't give away any points. Make her win them.

If you break her serve, great. If not, it's your serve.

Of course, the odds are 50-50 that you'll lose the racquet spin. In most cases, though, your opponent will choose to serve first, so you benefit either way.

PLAYING AGAINST BIG HITTERS

Power players are a fast-growing demographic in recreational tennis. Emboldened by the rapid technological advances in both racquets and strings and the bazooka-like groundstrokes on the pro tours, they come onto the court intending to blow you off the court.

To counter the power game, your best strategy is patience. Power hitters hit far more unforced errors than winners. If you keep feeding her balls, she'll lose more points than she wins.

Further, after the first few games, you'll become acclimated to her power and can counter it.

Finally, even nature works against the power hitter. As the match progresses, the balls will get fluffier, making them slower. And she'll get tired hitting all those balls back, further diminishing the weight of her shots.

Here are five tactics to take the sting out of the power hitter:

Take a step or two back. Until you get used to the pace, set up a little farther back behind the baseline. As you get your timing down, move forward.

Shorten your backswing. Use her power to generate your pace.

Focus on placement. Keep the ball deep. Forcing your opponent to hit from behind the baseline defuses her power.

Vary the spin and pace of your shots. Power hitters are often rhythm players. Changing the pace and location of your shots can throw her off. Soft slices and high shots can frustrate big hitters. Throw in the occasional lob.

Keep them moving. Power hitters are at their best when they can step into their shot. If you keep your opponent moving, either side-to-side or front-and-back, she won't be able to tee off.

PLAYING THE PUSHER

The pusher is one of the most common opponents you'll face at this level. He's the guy who gets everything back with nothing on it, forcing you to generate all the power, all the initiative, and—too often—all the errors.

Playing pushers isn't any fun because the foundation of their game is to frustrate you.

The biggest temptation when playing a pusher is to try to overpower him. After all, his ball floats across the net and sits up in the court, just begging to be pounded. That's exactly what he wants you to do. He's happy to block back your shots all day long, waiting for you to over-hit.

At the other extreme, you might be tempted to try to out-push a pusher. Don't bother. He's better at it than you are.

So what should you do?

Be patient. Accept that the points are going to last a while, because he's not going to give you the early unforced error. You'll have to earn the points, either by getting in position to hit a winner or putting him in a position to make a mistake. Keep hitting deep and safe.

Stay on your toes. Because the pusher's shots have so little pace, we tend to slow down. We become flat-footed and wait for the ball. You must do the opposite. Go get the ball. Taking the ball early minimizes the effects of the pusher's spins and disrupts his favored slow pace. The key here is not to get overly aggressive. You're not speeding up the pace of your shots; you're picking up the pace of the points.

Get to the net. Come in on any ball landing inside your service box. Hit your approach right at your opponent to deny him any angles. Word of caution: Pushers tend to lob well, so be ready to backtrack.

Bring him to the net. Change up your strategy every so often and draw the pusher to the net. As a general rule, pushers prefer to stay behind the baseline.

PLAYING THE LEFTY

About 10 percent of the population is left-handed, but lefties seem much more common among tennis players. Maybe they're drawn to the game because they have several significant advantages.

Right from the start, a lefty's serve gives her the edge. The ball spins in the opposite direction of right-handed serves; it can take several return games to get used to it. More challenging, when receiving in the ad court, a lefty's slice serve can pull you off the court; if you're right-handed, you can end up hitting a backhand return from outside the doubles alley.

A lefty also upends the basic shot pattern of hitting cross-court to the opponent's backhand. Instead, each of you will be trying to avoid getting on the wrong end of a forehand-to-backhand exchange. Because she plays a lot more righties than you play lefties, she's probably more adept at it.

To counter these advantages, you need to adapt your basic strategy when playing a left-handed opponent.

Take two steps to the left to return serve. The slice serve is often her best, so neutralize it by setting up a couple steps to the left in both the deuce and ad courts. You'll open yourself up to flat serves down the center, but make her prove she can hit it consistently.

Move forward on the slice serve. Even as you slide to the left, move diagonally forward to cut the ball off before it spins away from you.

Target the middle of the court. Our relative inexperience playing lefties tends to open up angles for their shots. To defuse this advantage, keep the ball in the middle of the court. While this may not seem like an adroit strategic move, any time you can limit your opponent's options, you improve your situation.

Ignore the open court trap. Lefties often set up to their backhand side to protect against the cross-court forehand. As a result, they leave themselves open to your down-the-line drive. Don't bite. Not only is the down-the-line shot risky, it's a trap. By force of circumstances, a lot of lefties have good running cross-court forehands.

Protect your backhand. Take a page from the lefty playbook and line up a step or two to the left to protect your backhand. Points with lefties often end up with their hitting forehands to your backhand. That's not a good situation. By taking a step or two to the left, you narrow their target area and can maybe even tempt them to take a chance and go down the line.

PLAYING THE NET RUSHER

Net rushers at the recreational level tend to throw us off our game. We encounter them so rarely that we aren't prepared for their aggressive style. As a result, they impose their game on ours rather than the other way around.

The net rusher compresses time on the court. First, he keeps the points short. When he serves and volleys, the point often ends within two or three shots. In your service games, he comes in at the first opportunity. You never have the chance to get into the rhythm of hitting your groundstrokes.

Second, the net rusher reduces the time you have to hit the ball. By moving forward, he shortens the court. The ball comes back at you sooner and carries more pace. You have to react quicker and hit sooner.

If you let the net rusher dictate the rhythm of the match, he'll be playing his A game and you'll end up way down the alphabet. Adapt your game just enough to defuse or disrupt his. Here's how to make that happen.

Attack the net. Taking the net gives you an immediate advantage, even if you don't have a strong net game.

Eliminate free points. When the net rusher comes in, ignore the urge to immediately hit a passing shot. Your better option is to keep the ball in play. Force the net rusher to hit a winning volley. Every time the ball is on your opponent's racquet, there is a chance he will make a mistake. You're always in the point when the ball is in play.

Aim at the net rusher. A player who lives at the net probably has better-than-average volleys. If you put the ball on his forehand or backhand, you're putting it in his wheelhouse. Instead, hit at him. Force him to move out of the way to get his racquet onto the ball.

Take away his time. The net rusher is good at reducing your time but often doesn't face the same challenge. Step up to—or even inside—the baseline to hit shots. Rob him of the time to get in a good position to hit a volley.

Bleed off the pace. Rather than ripping away at the ball, take something off it. Hit softer returns that drop below the top of the net. You force your opponent to hit up.

Lob. Any time the net rusher crowds the net, lob.

PANCHO SEGURA'S KEYS TO SUCCESS

In his book *Pancho Segura's Championship Strategy*, Segura provided an in-depth analysis of his strategic concepts. A championship player in his own right, Segura became a mentor to many of the top players in the 1970s and 1980s. He was renowned for his ability to break down his opponent's game and to impose his own strategy on the match. The book is no longer in print, but you can pick it up secondhand.

Many of Segura's keys to success apply to recreational players.

• Losers serve double faults.

• Losers have cannon-shot first serves and pat-ball second serves.

• Winners will only miss two or three returns of serve per set against other intermediates.

• Winners can consistently play to the opponent's backhand.

• Winners do not miss a setup.

• Losers come to the net without adequate preparation (or adequate overheads).

- Winners can hit forehands cross-court and backhands cross-court all day long; they only go down the line when the return is short or when they absolutely know the down-the-line shot will go in.

- Winners would rather poop the ball back, knowing it will at least go in, when they are pressed by a hard ball, rather than go for a big shot that has hardly any chance of going in.

- Winners play percentage tennis, making the most of their own strengths and the most of their opponent's weaknesses. If the winner has a weak backhand, he plays it only as a steady shot. If the winner gets a short shot to his backhand that he can run around, he takes it on his forehand.

- Winners keep track of their own losers, not their winners. A real winner knows how many backhand returns of serve he has missed after a match. There won't be very many, because, if his backhand return is failing him, he will lob, loop, or even kick the ball back in.

- Winners know that even if they miss two or three volleys in a row, it is still not necessary to stay in the back court every point. However, after losing three games by coming in and getting passed, the winner will change his strategy.

- The winner would rather win than look good; the loser would rather hit hard than win.

TEN BEST TIPS

An effective tennis strategy plays to your strengths and discovers and exploits your opponent's weaknesses. Your strategy must be basic and straightforward. The game moves too fast to keep track of an endless series of "If he does this, I'll do that" concepts. You're not putting together an NFL game plan. Keeping it simple and not trying to do too much will produce your best results.

Here are 10 components of a solid strategy for recreational tennis players. Although the components are complementary, fitting together to create a powerful and complete strategy, you don't need to implement all of them at once. In fact, it's better if you don't. Pick one or two that are close to your game right now and blend them in. When you feel comfortable, add one or two more. Don't disrupt your game. Let your strategy develop naturally. You will soon see improved results and you will have more fun playing.

Keep the ball deep. The foundation of any successful tennis strategy is hitting the ball deep into the court. Balls that land beyond the service line keep your opponent from taking control of the point. He can't power the ball past you or hit angled shots to pull you off the court.

Hitting shots past the service line may not seem sufficient, but you would be surprised at how many shots land inside the service box. As you become more comfortable, and when you have the time to set up, aim deeper. If you can develop some consistency in landing the ball about 10 feet from the baseline, you will keep most opponents from putting pressure on you.

Hit cross-court. In baseline rallies, hit cross-court. It's your best choice for two reasons. First, the geometry of the tennis court makes it your safest shot. The court is 4 1/2 feet longer on a diagonal from corner to corner than it is on a perpendicular from baseline to baseline, and the net is 5 1/2 inches lower over the middle than it is at the sidelines.

Second, cross-court shots limit your opponent's options. His correct choice is to return cross-court, where you are ready and waiting. His other choice is to go down the line, but that is a high-risk shot. Not only does he have to take into account the higher net and shorter court, but he brings the sideline into play.

Honor the ball's direction. Changing the direction of the ball significantly increases your risk of hitting an unforced error. Deflecting the ball to redirect your shot is inherently approximate. A slight miscalculation in the angle of the racquet face can send the ball outside the lines.

Changing direction also alters the geometry of the exchange, giving your opponent more options. If you open up your court, you'll end up having to hit on the run, which is more difficult.

As the shot count in a rally climbs, the urge to do something different can become overwhelming. Don't give in. Instead, hit the ball back the way it came and let your opponent surrender to temptation.

Prey on their weakness. Every recreational tennis player has a weak link that undermines his game. For most of us, that shot is the backhand, especially the high backhand. A strategic cornerstone is to figure out your opponent's weakness as soon as possible and relentlessly attack it throughout the match.

From the moment you walk on the court, during the warm-up and into the match probe your opponent's game for his weak link. It doesn't necessarily have to be a stroke; it could also be poor court coverage or faulty strategic thinking. Once you find it, attack it whenever you can. Don't worry that he will anticipate your shots. He won't be able to hurt you with his replies. (If he does, you're targeting the wrong thing.) Furthermore, don't be concerned that your pounding his weakness will help him improve it; match conditions aren't conducive to making sudden breakthroughs in our games.

A word of caution: In your assault on his weakness, don't increase your own risk. For example, in your fervor to lay bare his backhand, don't return his serve in the deuce court down the line. Instead, return cross-court and work the ball over to his backhand.

Attack the short ball. Recreational players hit the ball short. It's in our DNA. Fortunately, because your opponent probably won't be as focused on keeping the ball deep as you are, he'll most likely hit a short ball first. When that happens, attack and come in to the net.

Your best approach is to hit straight in front of you. It's the easier shot to hit and it puts you in center of your opponent's angle of reply. On the approach, most players hit a top-spin forehand and a slice backhand; hit whatever gives you a consistent shot. Don't try to win the point on your approach; it's a difficult shot because the court

is shorter and the net is more of a barrier. Instead, try to force your opponent into making an error or a weak return.

Even if your volleying isn't particularly strong, the percentages are in your favor when you control the net. Court geometry gives you a huge positional advantage. Your opponent's options are limited and he'll feel pressured to go for a winner. That combination breeds unforced errors.

If he gets the ball back, you have two options. When you can, put the ball away. When it's a tough volley, block the ball back and get ready for your next shot.

Bisect your opponent's angle of reply. On every shot during a point, get in the middle of your opponent's angle of reply, which is the area of the court into which your opponent can realistically hit the ball. If you're in the middle of that range, you should be able to get to almost every shot

An easy way to determine your optimal location is to mirror your opponent's position. If he's halfway between the center line and the sideline in his deuce court, you want to be in the same place in yours.

As the match progresses, adapt your court position to take advantage of your opponent's capabilities and tendencies. If, for example, he always goes down the line on his backhand, shade in that direction. Be aware that better players have wider angles of reply.

Get tough shots back no matter what. When your opponent hits a forcing shot that puts you on the defensive or on the run, ignore the temptation to go for a winner. Just get the ball back in the court. Force him to hit at least one more shot to win the point.

When you're out of position, the urge to hit a screamer down the line or whip a tight-angled shot cross-court can be powerful. You believe that if you don't win the point outright, you will lose it. Going for the winner, however, is a losing option. Maybe you'll hit in 1 out of 10 of those shots, but you're just giving away the other nine. Always make your opponent win the point. Even if all he has to do is hit an easy volley from the net, make him hit it.

In almost every instance when you're deep in the back court or outside the sidelines, your best shot is to lob. It's safe to hit and gives you the time to get back into position.

A deep lob that forces your opponent to backtrack to the baseline restarts the point. Even a short lob forces him to hit an overhead, which is not an easy shot for a lot of recreational players.

Get your first serve in. If you can get three out of every four first serves in, you will win most of your service games (as long as your first serve isn't a "patty cake" offering that allows your opponent to step in and tee off).

Your best option for getting a high percentage of your first serves in is to use your second serve. Spinning your serve at 75-percent power provides enough depth and pace to keep your opponent honest.

Target your opponent's weaker side on almost every first serve. In most instances, it will be his backhand. You limit his ability to hurt you with his return and increase his odds of missing. Again, don't worry about his anticipating your shot location.

Get every service return in. The server has significant advantages. Not only does she get to start the point, but she gets two cracks at it. Don't make it even easier for her by missing returns. Start each match with the goal of getting every return back into the court.

The key to effective service returns is to not try to do too much. Focus just on getting the ball back into play.

Return cross-court. Not only are you hitting the ball over the lowest part of the net, you aren't changing the direction the ball. Cross-court returns also limit your opponent's options; either he hits it back to you or he goes for the high-risk, down-the-line shot.

Emphasize depth over power. If you have time, add topspin to put some bite into your return. On harder serves, slice the ball to bleed the power.

Have a game plan. In a match between two equally skilled players, the player with a plan will win every time. When you have a game plan, you know how to maximize your strengths and minimize your weaknesses while at the same time negating your opponent's strengths and exploiting his weaknesses.

The best game plans are simple, such as: Hit every ball deep to the backhand. The key is to know what you want to do before you step on the court and then to do it.

Printed in Great Britain
by Amazon